Poems
that
do not
sleep

First published 2021 by
FREMANTLE PRESS

Fremantle Press Inc. trading as Fremantle Press
25 Quarry Street, Fremantle WA 6160
(PO Box 158, North Fremantle WA 6159)
www.fremantlepress.com.au

Cover images: Shutterstock, *war concept* by Zef Art; ABSFreePic.com,
    Beautiful star sky photo by Medilo.
Printed by Lightning Source.

 A catalogue record for this
book is available from the
National Library of Australia

ISBN 9781760990244 (paperback)
ISBN 9781760990251 (ebook)

 Department of
Local Government, Sport
and Cultural Industries

Fremantle Press is supported by the State Government through the
Department of Local Government, Sport and Cultural Industries.

Publication of this title was assisted by the Commonwealth Government
through the Australia Council, its arts funding and advisory body.

Poems that do not sleep

Hassan Al Nawwab

 FREMANTLE PRESS

Hassan Al Nawwab was born in Iraq in 1960 and came to Australia in 2003 with his wife and children. He is a poet and journalist who has published three volumes of poetry and two plays in Arabic and has received numerous awards for his poems. Al Nawwab has been a recipient of the Media Excellence Award in the Arab Media Day competition, and the international Al-Tayeb Salih Award for Creative Writing for his novel *The Kookaburra's Laugh*. He writes a weekly column for *Azzaman* newspaper, which is published in London and Iraq. This is Al Nawwab's first collection in English.

To my friends, the tramps and poets who preceded me to heaven, and left me alone, tormented by the memories that brought us together.

Contents

Diaspora

A poet sigh

I write scenes from life that the eye cannot see, as if I were trying to paint air or spirit. I write poetry as if I were creating a perfume of words, the poetry like the butterflies; I find it in my flowering heart, and the poem in which I do not smell the sweet and charming fragrance, I will destroy immediately. In my life I do not plan a moment to write a poem, and I do not write in a way of pseudo contemplation; poetry inhabits me like a jinn, and I can write the poem whenever I want, in the harshest of circumstances and even when darkness besieges my soul. There is a great flame that glows deep in my heart in perpetuity: in vain I try to extinguish it or rest from its burns a little bit, but still it shines and reveals more spiritual concerns. This journey is longer than the wars I fought, and the alienation I lived through. I want to be free, and my madness helps me with that; and this is what I will achieve before I leave life. This is the poetry in my perception, and through my long experience with pain.

Hassan Al Nawwab

شهقة شاعر

أكتبُ مشاهدَ من الحياةِ لا تستطيعُ العين رؤيتها؛ كما لو كنتُ أحاولُ رسم الهواءَ أو الروح. أكتبُ الشعرَ وكأنَّني أصنعُ عطراً من الكلمات، والشعرُ مثلُ الفراشات أجدها في قلبي المُزهِر، والقصيدةُ التي لا أشمُّ فيها الرائحة الزكيَّة والساحرة، سأدمِّرها على الفور. في حياتي لا أخطِّطُ لحظةً لكتابةِ قصيدةٍ، ولا أكتبُ بطريقةِ تأمُّلٍ زائفٍ؛ يَسْكُنُني الشعر مثل الجِنْ؛ ويُمكِنُني كتابة القصيدة متى ما أردتُ، في أقسى الظروفِ وحتى عندما يحاصر الظلام روحي. هناكَ شعلةٌ عظيمةٌ تتوهَّجُ في أعماق قلبي إلى الأبد: عبثاً أحاول إخمادها أو الراحة من نيرانها قليلاً، فهي ما فتئتْ تتألَّقُ وتكشفُ مزيداً من أسرار روحي. هذه الرحلةُ أطول من الحروبِ التي خضتها، والاغترابُ الذي أعيشُ فيه. أريدُ أنْ أكونَ حُرّاً وسيُعينُني جنوني في ذلك؛ وهذا ما سأحقِّقُهُ قبلَ أنْ أغادرَ الحياة. هذا هو الشِعرُ في تصوُّري ومن خلال تجربتي الطويلةِ مع الألمِ.

حَسَنْ النوَّاب

TREE FLYING

شجـرةٌ تطير

Fire

I saw the fire of war,
I saw the fire of women,
I saw the fire of poverty,
I saw the fire of prison,
I saw the fire of alienation,
I saw the fire of treason,
I saw the fire of insanity,
I saw the fire from God,
But
I did not see
Such a fire as that of poetry!
There is no
Fire like the fire of poetry!

نار

رأيتُ نارَ الحربِ،
رأيتُ نارَ النساءِ،
رأيتُ نارَ الفقرِ،
رأيتُ نارَ السجنِ،
رأيتُ نارَ الاغترابِ،
رأيتُ نارَ الخيانةِ،
رأيتُ نارَ الجنونِ،
رأيتُ نارَ اللهِ،
لكنْ
لمْ أرَ
أيَّةَ نارٍ مثل الشعر!
لا توجد
نارٌ مثل نارِ الشعر!

Theory

Life is wide
With a loyal eye
And it narrows
With the eyes of a traitor.

نظريَّة

الحياةُ فسيحةٌ
بعينِ المُخلصْ
وضيِّقةٌ
بعيونِ الخائنْ.

Stealing

In my country
Near the oil towers
People's homes are constructed
From clay.

سَرِقَةٌ

في بلدي
بالقربِ مِنْ أبراجِ البترولِ
تُشَيَّدُ منازلُ الناسِ
من الطينْ.

Deprivation

My country
Feeds babies
Fear, fire, and tears
Instead of milk.

حِرمانْ

بلدي
يُطْعِمُ الأطفالَ
خوفاً، ناراً، ودموعاً
بدلاً مِنَ الحليبْ.

Ammo

In the war
If the bombs are scarce
They put the soldiers
In the cannons!

ذخيرة

في الحربِ
إِذا شَحَّتْ القنابل
يضعونَ الجنودَ
في المدافع!

Cases

The soldier shivers in the first battle,
In the second he cries out of fear,
In the third, death becomes his friend.

حالات

الجنديُّ يرتجفُ في المعركةِ الأولى،
في الثانية يبكي من الخوفِ،
في الثالثة يصبحُ الموتُ صديقةُ.

Image

Above the mud house,
a fluttering red banner.
On her pole
stands a white dove
bleeding.

صورة

فوقَ بيتِ الطينِ
رايةٌ حمراء تُرفرفُ.
على ساريتها
تقفُ حمامةٌ بيضاء
تَنْزِفُ.

Fear

The soldier
Who committed suicide!
In front of me,
His fear was not because of war
But because his wife had left him.

خوف

الجنديُّ
الذي انتحرَ!
أمامي،
لمْ يكنْ خوفهُ منَ الحربِ
إنَّما بسببِ زوجتهِ التي هجرتهُ.

Flying

In the war,
I saw a tree flying!
From horror.

طيران

في الحربِ،
رأيتُ شجرةً تطيرُ!
من الرعبْ.

Forcing

You do not know
What is the soldier's sorrow?
When he holds a gun
Against his will.

إجبار

أنتَ لا تعرفُ
ما هو حزنَ الجنديِّ؟
عندما يحملُ بندقيةً
رغماً عنهُ.

Prayer

There is no benefit
From praying to God
When your heart
Is drenched with darkness.

صلاة

لا جدوى
من الصلاةِ إلى الله
عندما يكون قلبكَ
غارقاً في الظلام.

Why?

On the war front,
Thousands of soldiers,
I'm asking my self
Why am I among them?

لماذا

على جبهةِ الحربِ،
آلافُ الجنودِ،
أسألُ نفسي
لماذا أنا بينهم؟

.

Mother

When I absconded from the war, my mother came to visit me in prison at the end of the month. She came on the day for visiting prisoners, carrying food and a collection of books in a wicker basket I had asked that she bring me from my library. She and I barely got a place to sit in the courtyard of the prison, which was overwhelmed by the meetings of the families. In that moment, I felt that my life was like a grave without a witness. I said to her: Let me put my head in your lap so that I feel like I'm still in this life. When the prison guard kicked me, I awoke. My mother was not there. I was dreaming that she came, though she passed away years ago.

أُمْ

عندما هربتُ من الحربِ، جاءتْ أمي لزيارتي في السجنِ نهاية الشهر. لقدْ جاءتْ في يومِ زيارةِ السجناءِ، حاملةً الطعام ومجموعةً من الكتبِ في سلّةِ خوصٍ؛ كنتُ قدْ طلبتُ منها إحضارها من مكتبتي. بالكاد حصلنا أنا وهي على مكانٍ للجلوسِ في فناءِ السجنِ الذي ملأتهُ عوائلُ السجناء. في تلكَ اللحظةِ شعرتُ أنَّ حياتي كانتْ مثل قبرٍ بلا شاهدةٍ. قلتُ لها: دعيني أضعُ رأسي في حضنكِ حتى أشعرُ أنني ما زلت في هذه الحياة. عندما ركلني حارس السجن، استيقظتُ. لمْ تكنْ والدتي هناك. كنتُ أحلمُ أنها جاءتْ رغم أنَّها وافتها المنيَّة منذ سنوات.

Rope

In my homeland, the cord of honesty became too short.
In my homeland, the lying rope has become very long.

حَبْلٌ

في وطني أصبحَ حَبْلُ الصدقِ قصيراً للغاية.
في وطني، أصبحَ حَبْلُ الكذبِ طويلًا جدًا.

Wind

Who shakes the branches of the tree now?
You believe it is the wind,
But I say to you
In fact
It is my loud cry
And the wounded screams of my heart
For my country sinking
In bombshells and blood.

ريحٌ

مَنْ يهزُّ أغصانَ الشجرةِ الآن؟
أنتَ تعتقدُ أنَّها الريح،
لكنْ أقولُ لكَ
في الحقيقةِ
إنَّها شهقاتُ عويلي
وصراخُ جراحاتِ قلبي
على وطني الغارقُ
بالقنابلِ والدمْ.

Ash

The wicked soul
cannot fly to the sky
because his wings
have become ash.

رماد

الروحُ الشريرةُ
لا تستطيعُ أنْ تطيرَ إلى السماء
لأنَّ جناحيْها
أصبحا رمادًا.

Safety

Wars die
When the heads of killers
Become doves' nests.

أمانْ

تموتُ الحروبُ
عندما رؤوسُ القتلةِ
تصبحُ أعشاشَ حَمَامْ.

Drums

For the country
That does not beat the war drums,
Her homes are not ruined
And deprivation is not spread
Amongst her people.

طبول

البلادُ
التي لا تقرعُ طبولَ الحربِ،
لا تُدمَّرُ منازلُهَا
ولا ينتشرُ الحرمانُ
بينَ شعبِها.

Cabman

When the horse of the cabman died,
The carriage was neglected
And the family was without food,
So to rescue his family
From starvation,
And the carriage from oblivion,
He decided to become the horse for the carriage.

الحُوذي

لمَّا ماتَ حصانُ الحوذي،
أُهمِلَتْ العربة
وَغَدَتْ العائلةُ بلا طعامٍ،
ولكي يُنقذُ عائلتهُ
من الجوع،
والعربةَ من النِّسيانِ،
قرَّرَ أنْ يصبحَ حصانَ العربةِ.

Memories

The soldier who returned from war
Sleeps with his helmet
Because he still fears the enemy.
The soldier who returned from war
Looks like a fool to people
Because the whistle of bombs
Still reverberate in his head.
The soldier who returned from war
Arrived in Australia
And whenever he sits in a bar
Has a delusion that it is the last day of his leave.
The soldier who returned from war
Speaks in a whisper so the enemy cannot hear him.
The soldier who returned from war
A stranger, a stranger, a stranger.
Whenever he eats food
He remembers his comrades' bodies
Decomposing in no-man's-land
And nausea overtakes him.
The soldier who returned from war
Is tormented and wishes
That the war had eaten him.
The soldier who returned from war
Is haunted by nightmares
He sees his dreams rotting in a stagnant pond.
The memories of the soldier
Who returned from war
Will kill him.

ذكريات

الجنديُّ الذي عادَ مِنَ الحربِ
ينامُ معَ خُوذتِه
لأنَّهُ لا يزال يخشى العدو.
الجنديُّ الذي عادَ مِنَ الحربِ
يبدو وكأنَّهُ معتوهٌ للناسِ
لأنَّ صفيرَ القنابلِ
لا يزالُ يترَدَّدُ صداهُ في رأسِه.
الجنديُّ الذي عادَ مِنَ الحربِ
وصلَ إلى أستراليا
وكُلَّما جلسَ في حانةٍ
يتوهَّمُ أنَّهُ آخِر يومٍ في إجازتِه.
الجنديُّ الذي عادَ مِنَ الحربِ
يتكلَّمُ بصوتٍ هامسٍ حتى لا يسمعهُ العدو.
الجنديُّ الذي عادَ مِنَ الحربِ
غريبٌ، غريبٌ، غريبٌ.
كُلَّما أكلَ الطعامَ
يتذكَّرُ جُثثَ رفاقِه
تَتَفَسَّخُ في أرضِ الحرامْ
فيغلبهُ الغثيانْ.
الجنديُّ الذي عادَ مِنَ الحربِ
يتلظَّى ويتمنَّى
لو أنَّ الحربَ أكلتهُ.
الجنديُّ الذي عادَ مَنِ الحربِ
الكوابيسُ تطاردهُ
يرى أحلامَهُ تَتَعَفَّنُ في بركةٍ راكدةٍ.
ذكرياتُ الجنديُّ
الذي عادَ مِنَ الحربِ
سوفَ تقتلهُ.

Target

Every war –
Her only victory
Is human destruction.

استهداف

كُلُّ حربٍ -
انتصارها الوحيدْ
هو تدمير الإنسانْ.

No way

You
Possess all the bombs
And the guns
And we have only poems.
But all these weapons
Are not able to kill
A single poem.

مُستحيل

أنتَ
تمتلكُ كُلُّ القنابلْ
والبنادقْ
ونحنُ لدينا القصائد فقطْ
لكنْ كُلَّ هذهِ الأسلحة
ليستْ قادرةً على قتلِ
قصيدةٍ واحدةٌ.

Purity

Till
You triumph
Over desperation,
You must pray to God,
Every evening,
Talk with the moon.
And sing to the sun
Every morning,
Feed the birds,
And share your bread with the homeless,
Water the rosebushes,
And do not sleep before you ask yourself,
Have I been honest in my life today?

نقاء

حتَّى
تنتصرُ أنتَ
على اليأس،
يجبُ أنْ تُصلِّي إلى الله،
كُلُّ مساءٍ،
تحدَّثْ مع القمر.
وغنِّ للشمس
كُلُّ صباحٍ،
أطْعِمْ الطيور،
وتقاسمْ خُبزكَ مع المشردين،
أسْقِ شُجيراتِ الوردِ،
ولا تَنمْ قبلَ أنْ تسألَ نفسكَ،
هلْ كنتُ صادقاً في حياتي اليوم؟

Writing

In the trenches of war
I wrote about love only,
And when I survived
I began to write about death
That I saw there.

كتابة

في خنادقِ الحربِ
كتبتُ عن الحبِّ فقطْ،
وعندما نجوتُ
بدأتُ أكتبُ عن الموتِ
الذي رأيتُ هناك.

Steps

Let everything be silent!
All in all,
Everything!
The birds' chirrup
The lovers not exchanging kisses
Hymns and prayers
Shouts of the children
Songs of the people
The beat of the wedding drums
The dancing in the disco
The cars in the streets
The talk –
Let them be silent,
All in all,
Until we hear
The footsteps of terrorism
Fade into silence from the town.

خطوات

دَعْ كُلَّ شيءٍ يصمتْ!
الكلُّ في الكلِّ،
كُلُّ شيء!
زقزقةُ الطيور
العشّاق عنْ تبادلِ القُبلاتْ
الترانيمُ والصلاةَ
صيحاتُ الأطفال
أغنياتُ الناسِ
قرعُ طبولِ الزفافِ
الرقصُ في الديسكو
السياراتُ في الشوارع
الحديثْ-
دَعهُمْ يصمتونْ،
الكلُّ في الكلْ،
حتَّى نسمعُ
خُطى الإرهاب
تُهزمُ في صمتٍ مِنَ المدينة.

61

DIASPORA

شَـتَات

Tyrant

Because they could not bear
To see the devil chase them
With his baton and weaponry,
Refugees
Abandoned their country
Because the devil was chasing them
Even in their dreams.

طاغية

لأنَّهم ما عادَ بمقدورهم
رؤية الشيطان يطاردهم
بهراوتِهِ وسلاحهِ،
اللاجئون
تخلُّوا عن بلادهم
لأنَّ الشيطان كانَ يطاردهم
حتى في أحلامهم.

Reprimand

I am a tank driver,
I spent nine years in the war,
I never shot
But all bullets in the war,
As if it is now,
Crouch on my chest.

شَجْبْ

أنا سائقُ دبَّابة
قضيتُ تسعَ سنواتٍ في الحرب،
لمْ أطلقْ النارَ أبداً
لكنْ كُلَّ رصاصِ الحربِ،
كما لو أنَّهُ الآن،
يجثمُ على صدري.

Friends

Sometimes,
I am trying to remember,
The faces of my soldier friends,
But I just see
Candles flash in the dark.

أصدقاء

أحياناً،
أحاولُ أنْ أتذكَّرَ،
وجوهَ أصدقائي الجنود،
لكني أرى فقط
شموعاً تومضُ في الظلامْ.

Shelling

The war has stopped
Long years ago
So why are there bombs exploding,
Still banging in my head?

قَصْفٌ

الحربُ توقَّفَتْ
منذُ سنواتٍ طويلةٍ
فلماذا انفجارُ القنابلِ،
مازال يخبطُ في رأسي؟

Do not ask me

You didn't see the shell explode metres away from your feet,
You didn't see soldiers bleeding under the flares of the Enlightenment,
You didn't hear the bomb whistling before it fell near your trench,
You didn't bear a martyr under the bombing barrage,
You didn't drink swamp water from thirst,
You didn't eat grass from hunger,
You didn't miss seeing your family for two years,
You didn't shave your chin and dye your boot for ten years,
You didn't cook tea and food with gunpowder,
You didn't sleep next to a wounded soldier in the last breath,
You didn't write poems by the light of a lantern,
You didn't scratch your face with dust and war smoke,
You didn't wake at the roar of the cannons,
You didn't receive insults at the checkpoint,
You didn't know the pain of the last day of leave,
You don't know the counterattack,
You don't know night fighting,
You didn't know the panic of walking between mines,
You do not know the horror of fire in trench,
You don't know what a movement means after midnight,
You don't know that bananas in the language of war means
    matériel for tanks!
You didn't sit under the summer sun for more than seven hours,
You didn't ever see a battle in a storm and fog,
You didn't stand in the rain at dawn,
You didn't sleep in snow,
You didn't bathe in cold water in winter,
You didn't wash your clothes with rainwater,
You didn't hear hostile planes,
Their roar over your head just metres away
You didn't wake up at dawn to stand in the parade yard,
So do not ask me why I do not laugh or sleep,
And think that I am mad.

لا تسألني

أنتَ لمْ ترَ القذيفةَ تنفجرُ على بعدِ أمتارٍ من قدميكِ،
أنتَ لمْ ترَ جنودًا ينزفونَ تحتَ مشاعلِ التنوير،
أنتَ لمْ تسمع صفيرَ القنبلةِ قبلَ أنْ تسقطَ بالقربِ منْ خندقكَ،
أنتَ لمْ تحملْ شهيداً تحتَ وابلِ القصفِ،
أنتَ لمْ تشربْ ماءَ المستنقع مِنَ العطشِ،
أنتَ لمْ تأكلْ العشبَ مِنَ الجوعِ،
أنتَ لمْ تفتقدْ رؤيةَ عائلتكِ مُنذُ عامين،
أنتَ لمْ تحلقْ ذقنكَ وتصبغْ جَزْمَتكَ طِوالَ عشرِ سنواتٍ،
أنتَ لمْ تطبخ الشايَ والطعامَ بالبارودِ،
أنتَ لمْ تنمْ بجانبِ جنديٍّ جريحٍ في آخرِ نفسٍ،
أنتَ لمْ تكتبْ قصائدَ على ضوءِ الفانوسِ،
أنتَ لمْ تحكّ وجهكَ بالغبارِ ودخانِ الحربِ،
أنتَ لمْ تستيقظْ على هديرِ المدافعِ،
أنتَ لمْ تتلقَ الشتائمَ عندَ السيطرةِ،
أنتَ لمْ تعرفْ ألَمَ آخرِ يومِ إجازةٍ،
أنتَ لمْ تعرفْ الهجومَ المضادَّ،
أنتَ لمْ تعرفْ القتالَ الليلي،
أنتَ لمْ تعرفْ ذعرَ السيرِ بينَ الألغامِ،
أنتَ لمْ تعرفْ رعبَ النارِ في الخندقِ،
أنتَ لمْ تعرفْ ما تعنيهِ الحركةَ بعدَ منتصفِ الليلِ،
أنتَ لمْ تعرفْ أنَّ كلمةَ الموزِ بلغةِ الحربِ تعني عتادُ للدباباتِ!
أنتَ لمْ تجلسْ تحتَ شمسِ الصيفِ لأكثرَ مِنْ سبعِ ساعاتٍ،
أنتَ لمْ تشاهدْ معركةً في عاصفةٍ وضبابٍ،
أنتَ لمْ تقفْ تحتَ المطرِ عندَ الفجرِ،
أنتَ لمْ تنمْ في الثلجِ،
أنتَ لمْ تستحمْ في الماءِ الباردِ في الشتاءِ،
أنتَ لمْ تغسلْ ملابسكَ بمياهِ الأمطارِ،
أنتَ لمْ تسمعْ هديرَ طائراتٍ معاديةٍ فوقَ رأسكِ على بعدِ أمتارٍ فقطْ،
أنتَ لمْ تستيقظْ عندَ الفجرِ لتقفَ في ساحةِ العرضِ،
فلا تسألني لماذا لا أضحكُ ولا أنامُ،
وتعتقدُ أنَّني مجنونٌ.

Monologue

I was not alone,
In the diaspora,
With me was
Pain, stubbornness,
Longing, losses,
Memories, misery
Crying, songs, nostalgia,
And fields of hopes.
I was not alone.
Oh, my country.

مُناجاةٌ

لمْ أكنْ وحدي
في الشَتَاتِ،
كانَ معي
الألمُ والعنادُ،
اشتياقٌ وفقدانٌ
ذكرياتٌ وبؤسٌ
البكاءُ، الأغاني، الحنينُ،
وحقولٌ من الآمال.
لمْ أكنْ وحدي.
يا بلادي.

Frustration

After we arrived in Perth, we moved from a refugee residence in Mirrabooka to an apartment close to the city centre, and we had to rely on ourselves to purchase food. The morning of our first day in this apartment and before my children woke up for breakfast, my wife told me we do not have bread. I went out looking for a bakery, setting out in a street leading to the city centre. On the way I conquered my vague sadness, but tears began to draw torrents on my face when I discovered that I had brought my family to a far continent to search of bread, I do not know where to find it now, just like when I was at home struggling to get food for them in the years of war, so what has changed?

My strength suddenly collapsed, so I sat on the edge of the sidewalk.

I was breathing like a frog!

Some people gathered around me, they were surprised, how this stranger who is over forty years old was crying like a lost child.

This is not a poem, rather a gasp!

What do you say?

إحباط

بعدَ وصولنا إلى بيرث، انتقلنا من مسكنٍ للاجئينْ في ميرابوكا إلى شقّةٍ قريبةٍ من وسط المدينة، وكان علينا الاعتماد على أنفسنا لشراء الطعام. في صباح يومنا الأوّلِ في هذه الشقة وقبل أنْ يستيقظ أطفالي لتناولِ الإفطار، أخبرتني زوجتي أنّهُ ليس لدينا خبز. خرجتُ أبحثُ عن مخبزٍ، وانطلقت في شارعٍ يؤدي إلى وسطِ المدينةِ. في الطريق قهرتُ حزني الغامض، لكنّ الدموع بدأتْ ترسم سيولاً على وجهي عندما اكتشفتُ أنّني أحضرتُ عائلتي إلى قارةٍ بعيدةٍ للبحثِ عن الخبزِ، ولا أعرفُ أينَ أجدهُ الآن، تمامًا كما فعلتُ عندما كانوا في المنزلِ أكافحُ منْ أجلِ الحصول على الطعام لهم في سنواتِ الحربِ، فما الذي تغيَّر؟

انهارتْ قوّتي فجأةً، لذلك جلستُ على حافةِ الرصيفِ. كنتُ أتنفَّسُ مثل الضفدع!

اجتمعَ بعض الناسِ حولي، فوجئوا كيفَ كانَ هذا الغريب الذي تجاوز الأربعين عامًا

يبكي مثل طفلٍ ضائعٍ.

هذهِ ليستْ قصيدةً، بلْ هي شهقةٌ!

ماذا تقولْ؟

Wings

When I saw Kings Park
The first time
I felt that the sky was so close
It became my hat.
And I saw angels flying
There were feathers growing on my arms
I felt as though I was an angel
In Paradise
And could fly!

أجنحة

عندما رأيتُ حديقة الملوك
المرَّة الأولى
شعرتُ أنَّ السماءَ كانتْ قريبة جدًا
لقدْ أصبحتْ قُبَّعتي.
ورأيتُ ملائكةً تطيرْ
كان هناك ريشٌ ينمو على ذراعي
شعرتُ كأنَّني ملاكٌ
في الفردوس
ويمكنْ أنْ أطير!

Tears

In the homeland
We shed
The tears of expatriation
And in the exile
We became shed tears for
The homeland.

دموع

في الوطن
كُنَّا نذرفُ
دموعَ الاغترابْ
وفي المنفى
أصبحنا نذرفُ دموعَ
الوطنْ.

Morning

A wilted rose blooms with dew,
A sad bird tweets,
Loud music,
Heartache in a dark room,
Humming a tune for a song that he remembers.
Passers-by salute despondent,
Disturbing news,
Anonymous message in the mailbox,
Exhausted incense stick,
A molten candle,
Beer on an empty stomach,
Wind knocks on the door,
Smoking in an abandoned garden,
A book yawns and a bad cup of coffee,
Desperate poem in a newspaper,
A lukewarm smile
From an old neighbour who chats to herself,
A losing lotto card,
Deadly longing and memories that do not want to die,
Bag stuffed with dust,
An empty refrigerator except for coldness,
A cat over the fence of the house.
He is looking out from a dark window
To a faraway homeland.
This is a strange morning.

صباح

وردةٌ ذابلةٌ تزهرُ بالندى،
تغريدةُ عصفورٍ حزينْ،
موسيقى صاخبةٌ،
وجعُ القلبِ في غرفةٍ مظلمةٍ،
دَنْدَنَةُ لحنٍ لأغنيةٍ يتذكَّرُها.
المَارةُ يحيُّون اليائسين،
أخبارٌ مزعجةٌ،
رسالةٌ مجهولةٌ في صندوقِ البريد،
عودُ بخورٍ مُنطفئٍ،
شمعةٌ منصهرةٌ،
جعةٌ على معدةٍ فارغةٍ،
ريحٌ تقرعُ على البابِ،
التدخينُ في حديقةٍ مهجورةٍ،
كتابٌ يتثاءبُ وفنجانُ قهوةٍ سيء،
قصيدةٌ يائسةٌ في جريدةٍ،
ابتسامةٌ فاترةٌ
مِنْ جارةٍ عجوزٍ تتحدَّثُ مع نفسِها،
بطاقةُ نصيبٍ خاسرةٌ،
شوقٌ قاتلٌ وذكرياتٌ لا تريدُ أنْ تموتْ،
كيسٌ محشوٌّ بالغبارِ،
ثلاَّجةٌ فارغةٌ ما عدا البرودة،
قِطَّةٌ فوقَ سورِ المنزلِ.
هُوَ ينظرُ منْ نافذةٍ مظلمةٍ
إلى وطنٍ بعيدٍ.
هذا هُوَ صباح الغريب.

Yearning

The migrant
Remembers his homeland
More than the people who live in it.

تَوْقْ

المهاجرُ
يتذكَّرُ وطنهُ
أكثر من الناسِ الذين يعيشونَ فيه.

Nostalgia

The dress of an exile
Is nice and loose
But when night comes
It tightens and stifles
The body,
And in our dreaming
We miss the breeze
Of our country.

حنينْ

رداء المنفى
لطيفٌ وفضفاضٌ
لكنْ عندما يأتي الليلُ
يشدُّ ويخنقُ
الجسدْ
وفي حلمنا
نفتقدُ نسيمَ بلادِنا.

Similarity

The fireworks
Remind me of
Bombs exploding
Above my head
During the battles
When I was a tank driver.

تشابُهْ

الألعابُ الناريَّةُ
تُذكِّرُني بـ
انفجارِ القنابلِ
فوقَ رأسي
خلالَ المعاركِ
عندما كنتُ سائق دبَّابة.

Phobia

Even the buzzing bee
Makes me think
Of whizzing bullets,
Bombs whistling,
So how do I forget the war?

فوبيا

حتَّى طنينِ النحلةِ
يَدَعني أفكِّرُ
بأزيزِ الرصاص،
صفيرِ القنابلِ،
فكيفَ أنسى الحربُ؟

Difference

This exile
Resembles my homeland,
In goodness and feeling,
But the difference is
My homeland has become full of soldiers and bombs
And this exile has become full of angels and kisses.

اختلاف

هذا المنفى
يشبهُ وطني،
في طيبةِ القلبِ والإحساس،
لكنَّ الاختلاف
وطني أصبحَ مُمْتلئاً بالجنود والقنابل
بينما هذا المنفى أصبحَ مُمْتلئاً بالملائكةِ والقُبلاتْ.

Sneer

Please,
Do not despise these homeless people,
They have been in the past
Lovers
Wise men
Soldiers
Engineers
Writers
Artists
But luck let them down,
They became wanderers.
Do not laugh at them.

سُخريَّة

رجاءً،
لا تحتقرْ هؤلاءَ المشردينْ،
لقد كانوا في الماضي
عُشَّاقاً
رجالاً حُكماء
جنوداً
مهندسينْ
أدباءَ
فنانينْ
لكنَّ الحظَّ خذلَهُم،
فأصبحوا هائمينْ.
لا تضحك عليهم.

Wailing

Forty years
In my homeland,
I was crying,
And twenty years
In the diaspora,
I wipe the tears every day,
And still spilling.

نحيب

أربعونَ عاماً
في موطني
كنتُ أبكي،
وعشرونَ عاماً
في الشتاتِ،
أمسحُ الدموعَ كُلَّ يومٍ،
ولا يزالُ يَنْسَكِبْ.

Citizenship

For forty years
In my country,
I spent half of my age
In the war
Driving a tank,
I was wounded more than once,
But I did not get
First-class nationality!
The secret police watched me always,
Because my grandparents are from India.
When I arrived in Australia,
After two years, I obtained citizenship,
When someone asks me,
What is your nationality?
I say, I am an Iraqi,
But I don't have any original citizenship,
From my country,
Even now!

جنسيَّة

أربعونَ عاماً
في بلدي،
قضيتُ نصفَ عمري
في الحربِ
سائقُ دبَّابةٍ،
لقدْ جُرحْتُ أكثرَ منْ مرَّةٍ،
لكنِّي لمْ أحصلْ
جنسيةً من الدرجة الأولى!
كانت الشرطةُ السريَّةُ تراقبني دائمًا،
لأنَّ أجدادي مِنَ الهندْ.
عندما وصلتُ إلى أُستراليا،
بعدَ عامين، حصلتُ على الجنسيةِ،
عندما يسألني أحدُهم،
ما هيَ جنسيَّتُكَ؟
أقولُ أنا أنا عراقي
لكنْ ليس لديَّ أيَّة جنسيَّة أصليَّة،
من بلدي،
حتى الآن!

Owl

Inside your head
An owl,
Always hooting
Upon the ruins of the soul.
I shall kill him,
I shall silence him,
With my singing!

بومة

في داخلِ رأسكِ
بومة،
تنعقُ دوماً
فوقَ طُلُولِ الروحِ.
سوفَ أقتلُها
سوفَ أسكتُها،
بغنائي!

Confession

I am human, Muslim.
But I love Jesus a lot,
More than the Prophet Mohammed,
And the reason is Mohammed taught me
To defend myself by the sword,
While Jesus taught me
To defend myself by singing.
If one asked me now,
What is your religion?
I would tell them, I am Muslim
Without hesitation.
Yes, I respect Islam,
But I wish the prophet of my religion
Was Jesus.

اعتراف

أنا إنسانٌ مُسْلِمٌ.
لكنَّي أحبُّ يسوعَ كثيرًا،
أكثرُ منَ النبيُّ مُحمَّدْ،
والسببُ أنَّ مُحمَّداً علَّمني
الدفاع عنْ نفسي بالسيف،
بينما علَّمني يسوعٌ
الدفاع عنْ نفسي بالغناءْ.
إذا سألني أحدٌ الآن،
ما هي ديانتك؟
أقولُ لهم، أنا مُسْلِمٌ
بدون ترَدُّدٍ.
نعمْ احترمُ الإسلامَ
لكنَّني أتمنى نبيَّ ديني
لوْ كانَ المسيحْ.

Stars

When I retrieve the faces of my old friends,
Those who were with me in study and in war,
I don't see anyone in my memory,
Only green stars smile at me.

نجوم

عندما أستَرجِعُ وجوهَ أصدقائي القُدامى،
أولئكَ الذين كانوا معي في الدراسةِ والحربِ،
لا أرى أحداً في ذاكرتي،
سوى نجومٍ خُضْرٍ تبتسمُ في وجهي.

Homeland

I put my hand on your mouth,
It became a rose,
I put my hands on your eyes,
They became two stars,
I put my hands on your cheeks,
They became a peach garden,
I put my hands on your eyebrows,
They became two rivers of diamonds,
I put my hands on your brow,
It became a temple,
I put my hands on your neck,
It became a candle,
I put my hands on your breasts,
They became two holy shrines,
I put my hand on your heart,
It became my homeland.

وطنْ

أضعُ يدي على فمكِ،
يُصبحُ وردةً
أضعُ يدي على عينيكِ،
تُصبحانِ نجمتينْ،
أضعُ يدي على خدَّيكِ،
يُصبحانِ خميلتي خُوخٍ،
أضعُ يدي على حاجبيكِ،
يُصبحانِ نهرينِ مِنْ الماسْ،
أضعُ يدي على جبينكِ،
يُصبحُ معبداً،
أضعُ يدي على رقبتكِ،
تُصبحُ شمعةً
أضعُ يدي على ثدييكِ،
يُصبحانِ مزارينِ مُقدَّسينِ،
أضعُ يدي على قلبكِ،
يُصبحُ وطني.

Trembling

You can know the honest poem
If it enters your heart immediately
And your skin
Starts to shiver.

ارتعاش

يُمكنكَ معرفةَ القصيدةِ الصادقةْ
إِذا دخلتْ قلبكَ على الفور
وبشرتكَ
تبدأُ بالقُشْعَريرة.

.

Immortality

When
The poet dies
His body is buried in the earth
But his poems
Are buried in the hearts
Of all the people!

خُلُود

عندما
يموتُ الشاعر
تُدْفَنُ جُثّتُهُ تَحتَ الأرض
لكنَّ قصائدَهُ
تُدْفَنُ في قلوبِ
كُلِّ الناس!

Acknowledgements

Thank you to my friend Peter Jeffrey. My poems were unspoken until you gave them their tongues.

Thank you to my editor Georgia Richter. My poems looked like wild weeds, and if it weren't for you, they wouldn't look so elegant.

Thank you too to Sandra Mould, who has cared for me like a sister come down from the sky.

Printed in Australia
AUHW020817010921
351340AU00005B/5

9 781760 990244